For our Pops and Little Man

To Dr Abbott,
With endless gratitude for the gift of our lives... more time together. Love the Ganz family xoxo

Pops on Wheels

Written and Illustrated by
Nikki G. Stahl

Nikki G Stahl

NIK + JAX
PUBLISHING

Together we play
and work hard to get strong.
We squeeze the ball
and reach up high and long.

My Big Little Man,
I love watching you grow.
You're the joy of my life
just so you know.

Exploring with wonder,
WOW, look at you go!
My heart pitter patters.
You make the world glow.

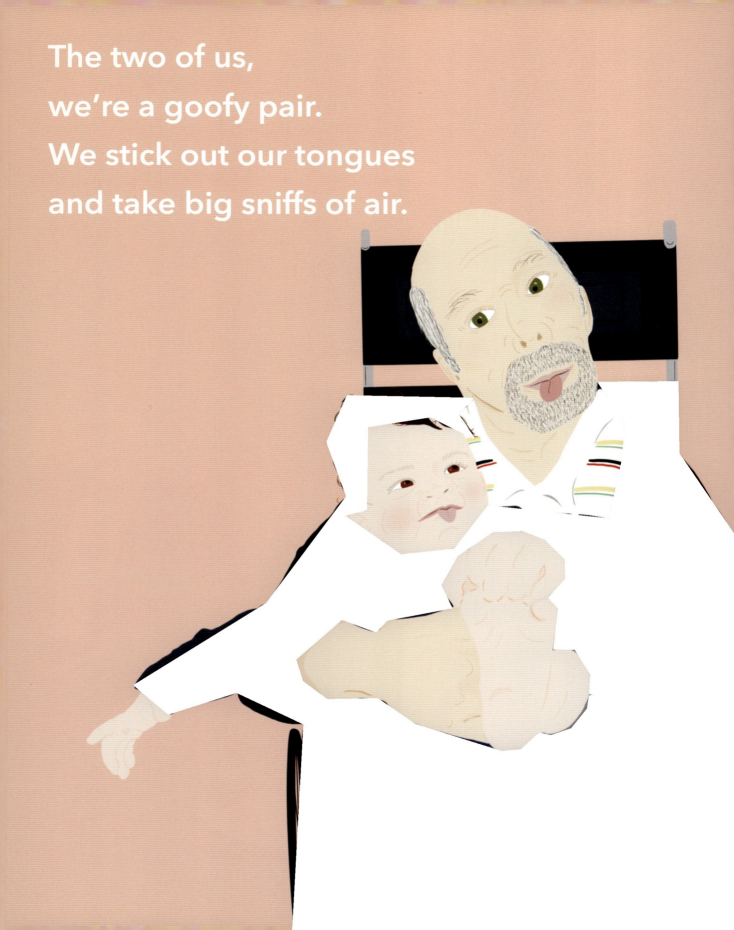

My Big Little Man,
I love watching you grow.
You're the joy of my life
just so you know.

Exploring with wonder,
WOW, look at you go!
My heart pitter patters.
You make the world glow.

Splishing and splashing,
we swim in the pool.
We both wear our floaties.
That's the number one rule.

After every fun day we tuck Pops into bed, where I climb over pillows to get to his head.

When everyone is quiet
and it's time to go to sleep,

we say sweet dreams moon
then sing soft as a peep.

My Big Little Man,
I love watching you grow.
You're the joy of my life
just so you know.

Exploring with wonder,
WOW, look at you go!
My heart pitter patters.
You make the world glow.

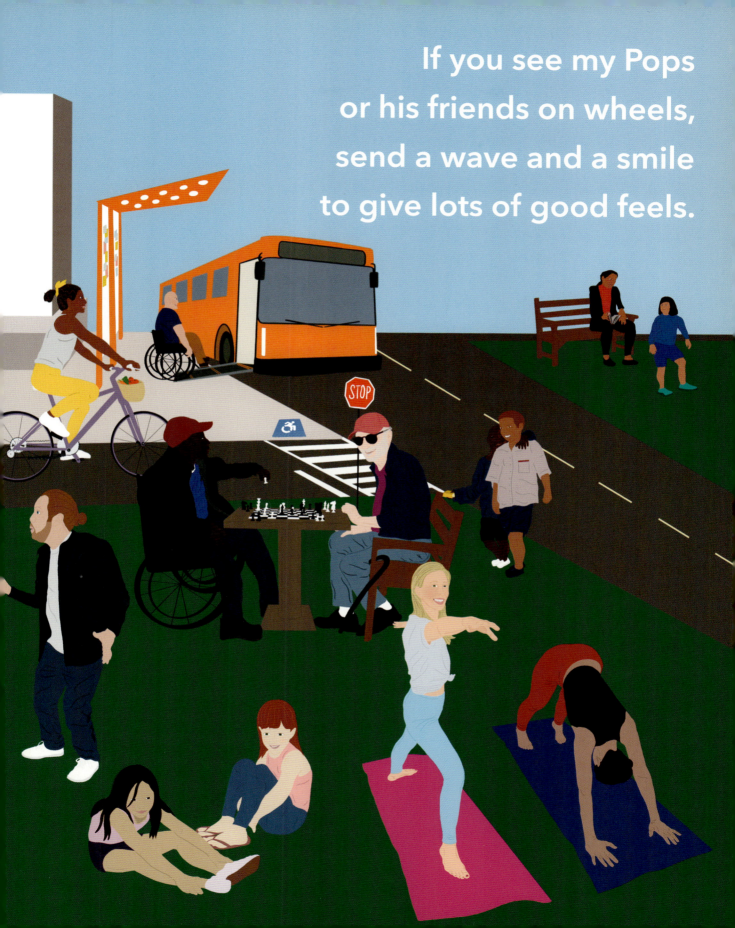

A Note from the Author

Several years ago our Pops had a stroke. In that moment we were given the gift of our lives: more time together. That time came with some adjustments including a wheelchair and a change in Pops' mobility. So, we relearned how to do the everyday, determined to continue living the way Pops always did, making each day the best day. This is our gifted time. We swim. We dance. We cook. We play. He escorted me down the aisle, and we danced at my wedding. He met his first grandson, who is the joy of his life, and is excited to welcome another. We continue to make each day the best, living life with love and compassion.
From my family to yours, we wish you all
the joy and beauty in the everyday
of this remarkable world.

Thank you for reading and supporting
POPS ON WHEELS.

Copyright © 2021 by Nikki G. Stahl. All Rights Reserved.
Published by NIK + JAX Publishing.
Printed in China by RR Donnelley.
This book was hand illustrated by the author.
Wedding photo credit to Courtney & Erin de Jauregui.

Special Thanks to the many friends, family, and medical professionals who have supported, loved and guided us along the way.

No portion of this book may be reproduced in any medium without the express written consent by the author. Please direct all inquiries and any requests for bulk purchase to: info@nikandjax.com

ISBN 978-1-7366784-0-4
First Edition Published 2021
Please visit our website for more information and supplemental teaching materials.
www.popsonwheels.com